Spring

Annalise Bekkering

WEIGL PUBLISHERS INC.
"Creating Inspired Learning"
www.weigl.com

Published by Weigl Publishers Inc.
350 5th Avenue, 59th Floor
New York, NY 10118
Website: www.weigl.com

Library of Congress Cataloging-in-Publication Data

Bekkering, Annalise.
 Spring : world of wonder seasons / Annalise Bekkering.
    p. cm.
 Includes index.
 ISBN 978-1-61690-046-5 (hardcover : alk. paper) -- ISBN 978-1-61690-050-2 (softcover : alk. paper) -- ISBN 978-1-61690-054-0 (e-book)
 1. Spring--Juvenile literature. I. Title.
 QB637.5.B45 2011
 508.2--dc22
                              2009050956

Printed in the United States of America in North Mankato, Minnesota
1 2 3 4 5 6 7 8 9 0 14 13 12 11 10

042010
WEP264000

Editor: Heather C. Hudak
Design: Terry Paulhus

All of the Internet URLs given in the book were valid at the time of publication. However, due to the dynamic nature of the Internet, some addresses may have changed, or sites may have ceased to exist since publication. While the author and publisher regret any inconvenience this may cause readers, no responsibility for any such changes can be accepted by either the author or the publisher.

Every reasonable effort has been made to trace ownership and to obtain permission to reprint copyright material. The publishers would be pleased to have any errors or omissions brought to their attention so that they may be corrected in subsequent printings.

Weigl acknowledges Getty Images as its primary image supplier for this title.

CONTENTS

What is Spring?

How do you know when it is time to put away your winter clothes? The weather warms, and the days become longer. This is the season called spring. Spring comes after winter and before summer. In parts of the world, winter snow melts and runs into streams and rivers. Plants grow, trees bud, and flowers bloom.

In North America, spring starts on March 20 or 21 each year. In South America, September 22 or 23 is the first day of spring.

6

Spring Science

What causes winter to change into spring? Earth travels around the Sun. Spring begins when the North and South Poles are the same distance from the Sun. On this day, the hours of day and night are almost the same.

Winter happens when parts of Earth are tilted away from the Sun. When spring begins, those parts of Earth tilt toward the Sun. The Sun rises earlier in the morning and sets later.

Starting the first day of spring, the Sun does not set at the North Pole for about six months.

Rainy Days

Have you heard the saying "April showers bring May flowers"? Rain is very common in spring. From roaring thunderstorms to a light drizzle, rain feeds plants and helps them grow.

Spring has many different kinds of weather. Once spring starts, the temperature begins to warm. Some days are hot, while others are cool. Hurricanes and hail are common in spring.

The largest known piece of hail was about the size of a dessert plate.

New Life

Why are so many baby animals born in spring? Many animals, such as bears, come out of **hibernation**. They search for food and mates. Birds that flew south for winter return to their northern homes to build nests and lay eggs.

Spring is when soil and air become warm enough for plants to grow. Spring rain and warmth help the seeds grow.

Some plants stop growing during winter. When spring comes, they begin to grow again.

11

Spring Events

Did you know that spring is a time to celebrate? Many special events happen in springtime each year. April Fools' Day happens on April 1. On this day, people play jokes on each other.

On April 22, people around the world celebrate Earth Day. It is a time when people think about ways to help the environment. This may include saving electricity, **recycling**, planting trees, or walking rather than driving. In 1970, 20 million people took part in the first Earth Day. Today, more than one billion people take part in Earth Day events.

Made for Mom

How do you show your mother you love her? Spring is a time to honor mothers. Mother's Day is celebrated on the second Sunday of May. Children give gifts, flowers, and cards to their mothers.

On Mother's Day in Japan, some children make their mother a meal that she taught them how to cook.

Happy Mother's Day

Eggs and Bunnies

Have you ever painted eggs at Easter? Easter is a **Christian** holiday. It also is a time to celebrate the beginning of spring. Easter happens on the first Sunday after the first full moon of spring.

The Easter bunny hides chocolate treats and painted eggs for children to find. Easter eggs and the Easter bunny are signs of the new life that comes in spring.

At Easter, the president of the United States hosts an egg rolling contest on the White House lawn.

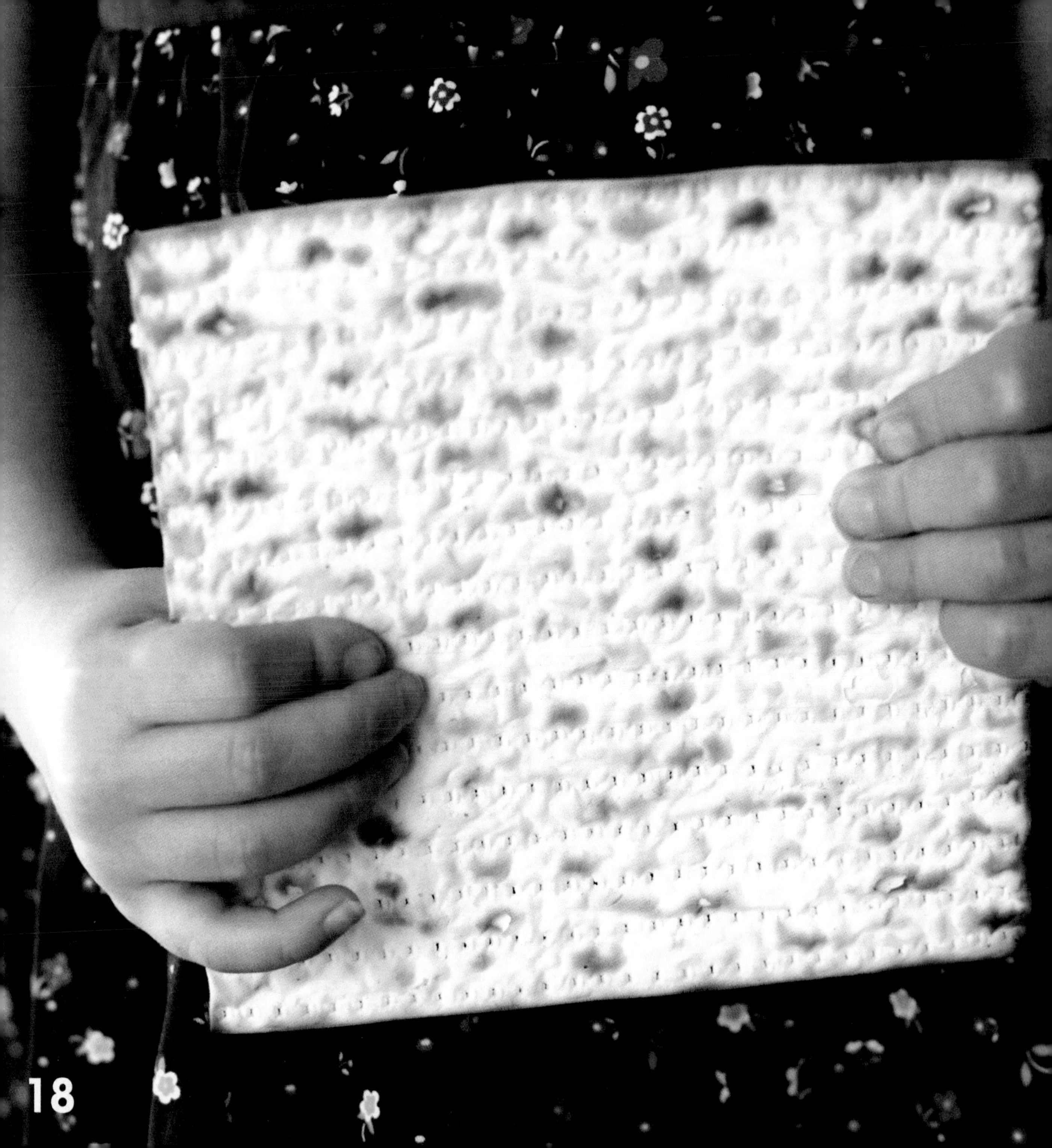

Passover

Did you know that a special Jewish festival happens in spring? Passover celebrates when Hebrew slaves were freed from Egypt.

God said the Egyptians would suffer 10 **plagues** if they did not free the Hebrew slaves. God told the Hebrews to paint lamb's blood on their doors so the tenth plague would "pass over" their homes. After the final plague, the Hebrews were freed from Egypt. They left Egypt in such a hurry that, if they were baking bread, it did not have time to rise. Today, unrisen bread is a symbol of Passover. This bread is called matzo.

Spring Stories

Does your family tell stories about special events? Some cultures have stories and legends about the first spring. This Ojibwa Indian legend explains the change of seasons from winter to spring.

Seegwun was the young spirit of spring. Peboan was the spirit of winter. Peboan's icy breath caused streams to stand still. Seegwun's warmth melted away Peboan and warmed Earth. Rain fell from Seegwun's hair. This made the flowers bloom.

Spring Seeds

Supplies

two plastic cups

water

paper towel

planting seeds, such as grass, wheat, peas, beans, and flowers

1. Soak the paper towel in water.
2. Put a sheet of paper towel in the bottom of each plastic cup.
3. Lay a seed on top of the paper towel in each cup.
4. Leave one cup on a window sill, where it will get plenty of light.
5. Place the other cup in a closet or some place that does not get much light.
6. Every day, check on the seeds. Make sure that the paper towel stays moist.
7. As the seeds start growing, what do you notice? Which plant grows faster? Why?

Find Out More

To learn more about spring, visit these websites.

Animal Planet
http://animal.discovery.com/
tv/spring-watch/spring-watch.html

BBC School Science Clips
www.bbc.co.uk/schools/
scienceclips/ages/5_6/
growing_plants.shtml

Planet Pals
www.planetpals.com/pdf
images/GB_Spring.pdf

World Almanac For Kids
www.worldalmanacforkids.
com/WAKI-ViewArticle.
aspx?pin=wak-302005

Glossary

Christian: a faith based on a belief in Jesus Christ and his teachings

hibernation: a period during which an animal is not active

plagues: diseases and acts that can cause harm, bother, or annoy a large group of people

recycling: using something again

Index

24